SADIST CINEMA

VOLUME ONE:
A SERBIAN FILM

Fwah Storm

SADIST CINEMA

A SERBIAN FILM

A VIDEOGEDDON Non Fiction Book

Edited By Dexter Williams

Cover Art & Design by Fwah Storm

This Book edition published in Great Britain in July 2015 by VIDEOGEDDON/Reload Entertainment

ISBN 13: 978- 1515170921

ISBN 10: 1515170926

www.videogeddon.co.uk

Print Edition July 2015

CONTENTS

INTRODUCTION

The history of cinema began with stirs of controversy. The kind of controversy that would spread through the grapevine, and in turn separate audiences before they had even laid their eyes on a single frame of a film. Moral panic and outrage over these films would become part of everyday conversation, and everyone had an opinion on them, regardless of whether they had seen them, or not.

A SERBIAN FILM

So, it goes without saying that controversy remained at the root of a lot of productions and releases of certain motion pictures throughout the decades to come. Even in today's society; where you can openly surf the internet and watch videos of beheading's, sick pranks, and happily share the notorious 'Two Girls One Cup' video with work colleagues through a group e-mail; There are still movies that cause members of the public to panic and aggressively boycott showings of these movies.

The list of controversial movies appears to be never ending, and as each year passes, more and more titles make the list. Some cause minor outrage, and others cause movie going audiences to be afraid of these films existence. But every now and then you get a movie that is both brave and transgressive enough that it causes the authorities to investigate its production crew, cast and film makers, accusing their art of being obscene and guilty of breaking various laws.

In this, the first book of hopefully many in the 'Sadist Cinema' series, we take a look at, analyse and explore the depths of one of these movies. A modern masterpiece that caused fear, moral panic and instant disgust in the eyes of many. That movie is none other than the notorious 'A Serbian Film'.

Needless to say, this book is not for everyone, and we will be discussing the films contents and the controversy it caused. Therefore there will be spoilers related to the movie, its story and its plot. However, this isn't just a warning about spoiling the movie for those of you who have not seen it before, but to also warn you that we will be discussing scenes from the movie that some will find offensive on many levels. This book

A SERBIAN FILM

does not exist in order for someone like me to judge the film makers and their actions, nor to judge them for putting disturbing and offensive scenes into their art.

So, if you are of a sensitive nature, and find it hard to read materials about disturbing themes, subjects and scenes from controversial movies, then please, return this book. Get your money back, and spend it on something else. I won't think any less of you for it. In fact, you would be earning a great amount of respect from me.

However, if you do enjoy learning about cinema, especially the more controversial entries from the history of cinema, then I sincerely hope you enjoy this book.

I have always been a fan of cinema ever since I can remember, and I have always had a special place in my heart for controversial cinema. It is always a pleasure for me to talk about controversial cinema on any level to those who will listen. So, thank you for listening.

Enjoy the book, and I hope to see you again soon for the next book.

Take Care, and stay awesome

F. Storm

WHAT IS A SERBIAN FILM?

'A Serbian Film' is horror thriller hybrid that was co-written, produced and directed by Srđan Spasojević. The film was produced in Serbia during 2010, and was the feature film debut from Srđan Spasojević.

The film tells the story of Miloš, an aging porn star who has found himself to be in financial difficulty after retiring from the sex industry. Unable to support his family, Milos is feeling the stress of trying to take care of himself, his wife Marija, and his son Petar.

However, Miloš is offered a part in an 'art-house' film, which would pay him handsomely, and in turn could put his financial difficulties to rest. After reluctantly agreeing to play a part in the film, Milos discovers that he is in fact taking part in a snuff film with child rape and necrophilic scenes and imagery.

The film featured a cast that mostly consisted of Serbian porn stars, most of whom were reluctant to participate in the film at first, fearing that it could jeopardise and destroy their careers. The cast for 'A Serbian Film' is as follows:

* Srđan Todorović as Miloš

* Sergej Trifunović as Vukmir

A SERBIAN FILM

* Jelena Gavrilović as Marija

* Slobodan Beštić as Marko

* Katarina Žutić as Jeca

* Ana Sakić as Jeca's Mother

* Lidija Pletl as Jeca's Grand Mother

* Lena Bogdanović as a Doctor

* Luka Mijatović as Petar

* Nenad Heraković as Keeper #1

* Carni Đerić as Keeper #2

* Miodrag Krčmarik as Raša

* Tanja Divnić as the Kindergarten Teacher

* Grace Slick as Herself

* Natasa Miljus as the Pregnant Woman

A SERBIAN FILM

'A Serbian Film' debuted on the art film circuit, and due to its graphic and relentless scenes that discuss many taboo subjects, it received a large amount of attention. Its graphic and violent scenes of rape, necrophilia and child sexual abuse caused controversy that had not been seen by any other movie.

The critical response was mixed at best, and after its debut 'A Serbian Film' had gained notoriety across the globe, earning itself several bans from multiple countries, heavy cuts made by other countries' censorship boards and federal investigations into the movie, it's makers and cast were under way (which we will discuss in more detail later on in this book).

DISSECTING THE MOVIE

Semi-retired porn star Miloš (Srđan Todorović) lives with his wife, Marija (Jelena Gavrilović), and six-year-old son, Petar (Luka Mijatović).

The opening scene of 'A Serbian Film' begins with a wide establishing shot of an alleyway outside of a bar as Miloš comes crashing out of the bar with a young woman draped all over him, kissing him passionately. This scene instantly makes you feel like you're watching a high budget porno, and as Miloš and his female companion begin to take of their clothes and start pleasuring each other, we cut to a close up of young Petar's shocked face as we discover that what we have briefly witnessed is one of Miloš' films being viewed by his six year old son.

This scene doesn't just show us a brief glimpse of what sort of a journey we have begun in choosing to watch the movie, but it also shows us that Petar is a metaphor for the audience member.

Miloš' brother, Marko (Slobodan Beštić), a corrupt police officer, is attracted to Miloš' wife, Marija. Marija is curious about her husband's past and is concerned about the family's income.

During the first act of the movie we are introduced to these vital characters, and we are shown a very brief glimpse at their current situation. However, while we focus on Miloš and his concerns about life, we are constantly reminded of young Petar.

Especially as he does what all young children do, and asks lots of questions. But Petar's questions are about how watching Miloš film had made him feel.

Shortly after the intial set of Miloš' home life and family situation we are introduced to Lejla.

Lejla (Katarina Žutić) is a former co-star, and upon catching up with Miloš, she offers him a starring role in an art film directed by Vukmir (Sergej Trifunović); an independent pornographer, who wishes to cast Miloš for his powerful erection. Having already caught Petar watching one of his films and unaware of the details of Vukmir's film, Miloš is hesitant to participate and continue his career, but eventually he reluctantly accepts in order to secure his family's financial future. While meeting Vukmir, Miloš passes a bald man and his entourage, regarding them warily.

A SERBIAN FILM

Filming begins at an orphanage, where Vukmir feeds Miloš instructions through an earpiece given by Vukmir's driver, Raša (Miodrag Krčmarik), all while a film crew follows him. Miloš sees a young girl, Jeca (Anđela Nenadović), physically abused and scolded by her mother (Ana Sakić), who has disgraced her deceased war hero husband's memory by becoming a whore. Miloš is then lead in to a dark room where screens show Jeca seductively eating an ice pop, while Miloš is fellated by a nurse. Then, Miloš is instructed to receive fellatio from the mother, while Jeca watches. Miloš refuses, but is forced to continue. Marko later informs him that Vukmir is a former psychologist and has worked in children's TV and state security. Vukmir meets a hesitant Miloš afterward to explain his artistic style of pornography, showing him a film of a woman giving birth to a new-born baby, which is then immediately raped by Raša, in what the director terms as "new-born porn". The disgusted and horrified Miloš storms out and drives away as Vukmir shouts to him. At a road junction, he is approached and seduced by Vukmir's female doctor.

A bloodied Miloš wakes up in his bed some time later with no memory of what has happened. He returns to the now abandoned set and finds a number of tapes. Viewing them on a blood covered video camera; Miloš discovers that he was drugged to induce an aggressive, sexually aroused, and suggestible state. At Vukmir's manipulative direction, Miloš beats and rapes Jeca's mother before decapitating her to induce rigor mortis and, later, a catatonic Miloš is raped by Vukmir's security. He then watches footage of Lejla voicing concern for Miloš, only to be restrained as her teeth are removed. A masked man then enters the room and suffocates her during fellatio. The footage continues as Miloš is led to Jeca's home, where an elderly woman praises him for killing her mother and offers Jeca as a

A SERBIAN FILM

"virgin commune". Miloš refuses and escapes through a window to an alleyway, where he watches an underage girl pass by as she is being pursued by a pair of thugs. He begins masturbating and is assaulted by the thugs before they are killed by Raša, who then takes Miloš back to a warehouse with Vukmir.

At the warehouse, Vukmir's doctor administers more drugs after which Miloš overpowers her, sticking the syringe into her throat. He is then taken into a room to have intercourse with two hidden comatose bodies under a sheet. As Miloš is guided onto one body, the masked man from Lejla's film enters and begins raping the other. Vukmir then reveals the masked man to be Marko, his victim to be Marija, and finally, that Miloš is raping Petar. An enraged Miloš lunges at Vukmir and smashes his head against the floor, initiating a brawl during which Marija bludgeons Marko to death with

A SERBIAN FILM

a sculpture. Miloš wrestles a gun from a guard and shoots everyone except his family and the one-eyed Raša, whom he kills by ramming his erect penis into his empty eye socket. A dying Vukmir praises Miloš' actions as truly worthy of film.

Miloš, having recalled his actions, including locking his wife and son in their basement before passing out earlier, returns home to find them. He and his wife agree that they and their son should die together, so the three gather in bed and embrace before Miloš fires a fatal shot through himself, Petar, and Marija.

Sometime later, a new film crew, including the bald man from the beginning of the film, enters the bedroom. One of the security guards begins to unzip his pants and the director, the unnamed bald man, advises him to "start with the little boy".

A SERBIAN FILM

This description of the story and plot to 'A Serbian Film' is basic, but still covers a lot of major factors that not only moved the story forward, but also raised concern. Especially as some of the cast members were minors. However, it was revealed at a later date that during the production of the film that the young actors who portrayed Jeca & Petar were not present during the filming of certain shots, and that the film was cut in a manor in order to simulate their presence in the scenes.

The most notorious scene from the movie that is often discussed or used as point of contention is obviously the 'new-born porn' scene. However, the scene is usually discussed out of context, and is overly simplified. Especially from movie goers who have never seen the movie, but wish to use this scene as a good reason to not watch the movie.

While this is understandable, as no sane person willingly wants to view a scene of a new born baby being raped, it is still important to discuss this scene objectively. For instance; The usual remarks about the scene goes along the lines of 'Then two of the characters watch a film of a new born being raped, and call it new-born porn'. This of course sounds extremely vulgar, revolting and axiomatic.

However, an important piece of information is missing from statements like these. The simple fact that while Vukmir, The antagonist of the story, is clearly happy with viewing the film, Milos is horrified and disgusted by what he sees, and in turn storms out of Vukmir's office with every intention of putting a stop to Vukmir's awful schemes.

Yes, the scene is still disturbing and revolting, 'because it's meant to be. But it is not a pointless scene. Especially when you embrace the political undertones of the movie, and accept that Vukmir is an allegory of the Serbian government, in the eyes of the director, and that Milos is a representation of the Serbian public.

'A Serbian Film' is extremely well produced, and looks like the high budget foreign production, when in fact it was made on a shoe string budget.

The director had clear intentions with the movie, and all of his goals were clearly met in the final cut of the film. Which is a very brave feature that truly understands the meaning of pushing the envelope, and is more of a transgressive piece of art, and not just a studio made production.

The look of the movie is very sleek and well presented. The cinematography has been cleverly thought out in order to bring to life important scenes and subject matters while working under such strict requirements

A SERBIAN FILM

'A Serbian Film' is more than just a director trying to shock audiences for the sake of shocking them. It's a movie with an important message, and a strong voice that often goes unheard in this noisy world. So does the only thing it can do; It shouts as loud as it can.

'A Serbian Film' is a clever masterpiece of cinema that is not afraid of being relentless. It is well crafted, well structured, beautifully scored with an interesting blend of dub step and classical styled music scoring, and an all-round well-made movie.

It is not surprising that at all that it has caused moral panic and fear among movie going audiences, but the ostracising it receives because of this is truly unfair and unwarranted.

RECEPTION

The first ever showing of A Serbian Film took place on March 15th 2010 at midnight in Austin, Texas. During the introduction by Alamo Draft House Cinema's owner, Tim League, the audience in the theatre was once again warned about the extreme nature of the scenes they were about to see and given one last chance to leave the screening. He also encouraged a handful of audience members to join him on the stage where they jointly snorted lines of salt, squeezed lime juice into their eyes and took shots of tequila in order to "understand what Serbians have been through to create a culture of A Serbian Film". The following day, the film played once more.

On June 11th 2010 the film screened in Serbia, as part of the Cinema City festival in Novi Sad. The film then ran from July 16th to July 19th 2010 during the Fantasia Festival in Montreal as part of the Subversive Serbia program.

The film was then due to screen on August 29th 2010 at the Film Four Fright Fest in London, UK, but was pulled by the organizers following the intervention of Westminster Council. Films shown at the Film four Fright Fest Festival are usually shown pre-certificate, but in this case Westminster Council refused to grant permission for its exhibition until it had been classified by the BBFC.

A SERBIAN FILM

Following its DVD submission to the BBFC (as there were no theatrical materials available in the time frame requested for a proper theatrical classification), 49 cuts totalling four minutes and eleven seconds were requested for DVD certification. The UK distributor, Revolver Entertainment, initially looked into the possibilities of the process, but it became clear that the film would then have to be resubmitted to the BBFC and further cuts may then have been required.

It was decided that to show a heavily edited version was not in the spirit of the festival, and consequently its exhibition was pulled from the schedule. The film was replaced at the festival by Rodrigo Cortés' Buried starring Ryan Reynolds.

This was not the only UK screening of 'A Serbian Film' that was delayed or cancelled.

'A Serbian Film' was scheduled to be shown at the British Horror Film Festival in Bournemouth, UK. The Bournemouth

A SERBIAN FILM

Council approved the festival to show any film they wanted to show, as the event is strictly for over 18's only.

But a few days after Bournemouth Council approved the screening they changed their minds, and announced that' A Serbian Film' would only be approved to be shown once it was certified by the BBFC.

The festival director, Stuart Brennan, issued the following statement: "This is an unfortunate situation for us to be in. We believe strongly the film should be shown, however this new demand has left us in a position where we are left with little choice but to remove the film from our line up, as we cannot guarantee the film will be certified in time."

A statement concerning the matter of the Bournemouth screening was issued on behalf of Revolver Entertainment Ltd, the UK

distributor for the film, which read:
"Revolver Entertainment Ltd. has decided
with regret to withdraw 'A Serbian Film'
from exhibition at the forthcoming British
Horror Film Festival in Bournemouth. The
film has been submitted to the British Board
of Film Classification but does not, as yet,
have a confirmed 18 certificate. While the
film and any potential cuts are still under
review the film cannot be screened as per
the council's decision"

'A Serbian Film' had been nominated for
"Best Feature Film" and "Best Actor" for
Srdjan Todorovic at the festival award
ceremony. Festival director Stuart Brennan
commented on the awards ceremony that
had planned as part of his festival saying that
"Due to the awards being judged on the day,
the film that replaces 'A Serbian Film' will
automatically be nominated in the
categories that 'A Serbian Film' was
nominated for. It's a huge shame and a big
blow for our festival. But we do have a

A SERBIAN FILM

number of other great screenings, including a number of excellent film makers in attendance to discuss their films."

The Raindance Film Festival picked up the film at the Cannes Film Festival in May 2010, and subsequently held the UK premiere and "found a way around the ban by billing the screening as a 'private event'". The Sun tabloid described the film as 'sick' and 'vile' following the festival's 2010 Press Launch, and Westminster Council requested to monitor the invitations to the screening. The 35mm print was shipped from the BBFC for the October 8th 2010 premiere.

On October 21st 2010, the film had a single screening at Toronto's Bloor Cinema. It took place as part of the monthly event called Cinemacabre Movie Nights organized by Rue Morgue magazine. The publication also spotlighted the film and featured it on its cover.

On November 26th 2010, the film was refused classification by the Australian Classification Board, banning sales and public showings of the film in Australia. However, on April 5th 2011, the Australian Classification Board approved a censored version of the film. Later in 2011, the censored version was also re-refused classification after review.

On July 12th and July 16th 2011, the film was screened at FANTASPOA in Porto Alegre, Brazil and at least at one other film festival in the country, before being banned just before a screening in Rio de Janeiro. Initially the ban applied only in Rio, but afterwards the decision became valid throughout the country, pending further judgement of the film.

In March 2011, 'A Serbian Film' won the Special Jury Prize in the 31st edition of Fantasporto, Portugal's biggest film festival, in Porto.

On September 24th 2010, 'A Serbian Film' was released uncensored (104 minutes) in Serbian theatre's, with screening times scheduled late at night.

The film had a limited release in UK theatre's on December 10th 2010 in the edited form (99 minutes), with four minutes and eleven seconds of its original content removed by the British Board of Film Classification due to "elements of sexual violence that tend to eroticize or endorse sexual violence."

'A Serbian Film' thus became the most censored cinema release in Britain since the

A SERBIAN FILM

1994 Indian film 'Nammavar' which had five minutes and eight seconds of its violent content removed.

The movie had a limited release in the United States on May 6th 2011, edited to 98 minutes with an NC-17 rating. It was released on VOD at the website FlixFling on the same day, except only slightly edited to 103 minutes.

'A Serbian Film's North American DVD and Blu-ray release was on October 25th 2011 through Invincible Pictures. Netflix refused to carry the film as well as wholesale outlets Ingram and VPD.

Through Invincible Pictures, a limited edition uncut version was released via DVD on May 22nd 2012. Tom Ashley, CEO of the distribution company, commented on the release saying "Of course we would have preferred an uncut release last year. Unfortunately, the charges brought against Mr. Sala [director of the Sitges Film Festival] were something we had to seriously factor into that release. Now that those charges have been dropped, we can bring A Serbian Film to its fans as its director had intended."

The film was released to great controversy over its portrayal of sexual violence. Spasojević has responded to the controversy with "This is a diary of our own molestation by the Serbian government... It's about the monolithic power of leaders who hypnotize you to do things you don't want to do. You have to feel the violence to know what it's about."

While acknowledging some level of conservatism among the public and theatre owners, Spasojević says that government enforced censorship in Serbia is non-existent, and was not the driving force behind the making of 'A Serbian Film' : "In Serbia we don't have ratings, there is no law forbidding anything from being shown in a film and there is no law forbidding anyone from buying a ticket."

Blic 's Milan Vlajčić penned a middle-of-the-road review, praising the direction, technical aspects, "effective iconography", and "video game pacing" while saying that the film was taken to the edges of self-parody.

Đorđe Bajić and Zoran Janković of the web magazine Popboks gave the film a highly affirmative review, summing it up as "the dark Grand Guignol that shreds its celluloid victims with unconcealed intensity while showing in full colour and detail, the collapse of the last bastions of decency, morality, and rationality" and concluding that "it has a lot to say outside of the mere and unrestrained exploitation."

A SERBIAN FILM

In an interview, Serbian actor and film director Dragan Bjelogrlić criticized the film, saying that he thought it was "Shallow and plain wrong — sum up my feelings about this movie. I have a problem with A Serbian Film. Its director in particular. I've got a serious problem with the boy whose father got wealthy during the 1990's — nothing against making money, but I know how money was made in Serbia during the 1990's — and then pays for his son's education abroad and eventually the kid comes back to Serbia to film his view of the country using his dad's money and even calls the whole thing A Serbian Film. To me that's a metaphor for something unacceptable. The second generation comes back to the country and using the money that was robbed from the people of Serbia, smears the very same people by portraying them as the worst scum of the earth. You know, when the first generation of the Rockefellers finished robbing America, the second one built museums, galleries, charitable organizations,

A SERBIAN FILM

and financed America. But in Serbia we're seeing every segment of society continually being taken apart and for me this movie is a paradigm of that. I've never met this kid and I really don't want to since that meeting wouldn't be pleasant at all."

Based on 26 reviews collected by the film review aggregator Rotten Tomatoes, 46% of critics gave 'A Serbian Film' a positive review, with an average rating of 5.2 out of 10.

A. O. Scott of the New York Times wrote in his review, "At first glance—and few are likely to dare a second—it belongs in the high-concept shock-horror tradition whose most recent and notorious specimen is probably The Human Centipede. As is often the case with movies like this, A Serbian Film revels in its sheer inventive awfulness and dares the viewer to find a more serious layer of meaning."

A SERBIAN FILM

Karina Longworth of the Village Voice gave the movie an extremely negative review, calling the film "a passionate argument against a no-holds-barred exploration of extreme human sexuality and violence" and referring to the film's supposed commentary on the sad state of post-Milošević Serbian society as "specious lip service." She concludes: "That this film exists at all is a more cogent commentary on the nation's collective trauma than any of the direct statements or potential metaphors contained within."

A more critical review came from Alison Willmore, who said "Movies can use transgressive topics and imagery toward great artistic resonance. They can also just use them for pure shock/novelty/boundary-pushing, which is where I'd group Serbian Film. That it comes from a country that's spent decades deep in violent conflict, civil unrest, corruption and ethnic tensions makes it tempting to read more into the film than I think it actually offers—ultimately, it has as much to say about its country of origin as [Eli Roth's] Hostel does about America, which is a little, but nothing on the scale its title suggests."

Ain't It Cool News' Harry Knowles lists 'A Serbian Film' in his Top 10 films of 2010, stating "This is a fantastic, brilliant film – that given time, will eventually outgrow the absurd reactions of people that think it is a far harder film than it actually is."

Time Out New York's Joshua Rothkopf was very critical. He accuses 'A Serbian Film' of pandering to "mouth breathing gore hounds who found Hostel a bit too soft (i.e., fanatics who would hijack the horror genre into extremity because deeper thinking is too hard)" before concluding that "the movie says as much about Eastern Europe as Twilight does about the Pacific Northwest."

Tim Anderson of horror review site Bloody Disgusting attempted to dissuade anyone reading his review from ever seeing the movie. He wrote: "If what I have written here is enough to turn your feelings of wonder into a burning desire to watch this monstrosity, then perhaps I haven't been clear enough. You don't want to see Serbian Film. You just think you do."

In his very negative review of 'A Serbian Film', BBC Radio 5 Live's Mark Kermode called it a "nasty piece of exploitation trash in the mould of Jörg Buttgereit and Ruggero Deodato", going on to add that "if it is somehow an allegory of Serbian family and Serbian politics then the allegory gets lost amidst the increasingly stupid splatter."

A SERBIAN FILM

Furthermore, he mentioned A Serbian Film again in his review of Fred: The Movie, pairing the two as his least favourite viewing experiences of the year.

Calum Waddell of Total Sci-Fi in a negative review took issue with the filmmakers' statements that their film says something about the politics of Serbia, writing, "if you want to learn about Serbia, chances are, you won't be watching a movie whose main claim to fame is that a man rapes a new-born baby", before concluding that "Srđan Spasojević will go to his grave being known as the guy who filmed a grown man having sex with a baby. And that's something that – despite all of the money, attention and champagne parties at Cannes – I would never want on my conscience. Good luck to him in regaining some humanity."

A SERBIAN FILM

Total Film awarded the film two stars out of five, finding the film's shock hype was not fully deserved. They wrote "a film that was slightly silly and none-too-distressing to begin with. Works best as a reflection on modern day porn's obsession with masochism and humiliation."

42 | P a g e

CONTROVERSY

Shortly after its official release, 'A Serbian Film' caused a large amount of controversy across the globe. The movie was banned in Spain, Finland, Portugal, France, Germany, Australia, New Zealand, Malaysia, Singapore, Norway, and was temporarily banned in Brazil.

In September 2011, without any explanation, the movie was pulled from

Netflix's list of available titles, and from their in-site search results.

    In Spain 'A Serbian Film' was banned by a court in San Sebastián, Spain for "threatening sexual freedom" and thus could not be shown in the XXI Semana de Cine Fantástico y de Terror (21st Horror and Fantasy Film Festival). The film was shown at an adults-only screening at the Spanish Sitges Film Festival during October 2010. As a result, the festival's director Ángel Sala was charged with exhibiting child pornography by the Spanish prosecutor who decided to take action in May 2011 after receiving a complaint from a Roman Catholic organization over a pair of scenes involving the rapes of a young child and a new-born. The charges were later dropped.

A SERBIAN FILM

Upon initial release in Germany, the FSK (German motion picture rating organization) refused to give the film any classification at all, because there were concerns that the content may violate German federal law. However, on 30 June 2011, a cut version was published, where all offensive material was removed. This version was 13 minutes shorter than the original and was rated "No release to youths" which is also known as '18'.

The film was banned in Norway after two months of sales due to violation of criminal law sections 204a and 382 which deal with the sexual representation of children and extreme violence.

The film was temporarily banned for screening in Brazil. Although the film was given a "not recommended for those under

A SERBIAN FILM

the age of 18, due to depictions of sex, paedophilia, violence and cruelty" rating by the Dejus, a legal decision banned it temporarily due to its content "offending the government of Brazil". This was the first time a film was banned in Brazil since the promulgation of the 1988 Constitution. In July 5, 2012, this decision was overturned.

'A Serbian Film' is currently banned in Australia. Before its release, major Australian DVD retailer JB Hi-Fi announced that they would not be distributing the film, either online or in physical stores. They attributed this to the "Disturbing content of the film" and to a disagreement with the (then) R-rating. However, the film was available from this retailer for a time.

A SERBIAN FILM

It was refused classification and thus effectively banned in South Australia just days before its release date.

On September 19th 2011, the Australian Classification Review Board also rated the film "Refused Classification", effectively banning the film from distribution Australia-wide. According to the Review Board, "A Serbian Film could not be accommodated within the R18+ classification as the level of depictions of sexual violence, themes of incest, and depictions of child sexual abuse in the film has an impact which is very high and not justified by context." On 25 May 2012, the film was banned outright by the New Zealand Office of Film & Literature Classification.

On August 24th 2012, the film was rejected and banned without question by the Film Censorship Board of Malaysia. On the same day, it was banned in Singapore due to its content being "likely to cause controversy in Singapore".

Surprisingly, 'A Serbian Film' was not banned outright in the United Kingdom. However, that did not stop the movie from having issues upon its release.

Here is what the BBFC have said about their classification decision surrounding 'A Serbian Film':

'A Serbian Film' was initially submitted to the BBFC for DVD and Blu-Ray release on August 10th 2010. At the time, the film was scheduled to be shown at the London Fright Fest on August 29th 2010. Normally, the Fright Fest operates under a special agreement with the local licensing authority, in this case Westminster Council, allowing films that have not yet been classified by the BBFC to be screened without a certificate to an adults-only audience. However, rumours about the film's extreme content had led to Westminster Council receiving complaints about the proposed screening, as a result of which they took the unusual step of directing that the film could only be screened at the festival if it had been classified by the BBFC. The BBFC therefore needed to arrive at a decision on a potentially difficult and controversial film within nineteen days, if the Fright Fest screening was to proceed as planned.

Accordingly, the film was examined for the first time on August 13th 2010. Given the film's reputation and the need to arrive at a decision as soon as possible, the film was viewed by two examiners, plus the two Senior Examiners. Following this, the film was also seen by the BBFC's Head of Policy, the Director, the Vice Presidents and the President. In addition, a further screening was arranged so that other examiners could have an opportunity to see the film and express their views. As is normal with such a contentious feature, there were a range of views expressed about the film and the extent to which it conflicted with the Board's published Guidelines and classification policies.

Ultimately, however, it was concluded that numerous cuts would be required before the film could be classified at 18. The main issues for the BBFC were scenes of sexual and sexualised violence and scenes juxtaposing images of sex and sexual violence with images of children. Although the film makers had clearly taken trouble to avoid exposing any of the young actors to anything disturbing or indecent, and had offered to show the BBFC evidence of the dummy props used in the film's most difficult scenes, the BBFC's Guidelines nonetheless caution that 'portrayals of children in a sexualised or abusive context' may require compulsory cuts.

A SERBIAN FILM

On August 25th 2010, the BBFC presented
the film's distributor with a cuts list. In total,
49 individual cuts were required, across 11
scenes. It was estimated that around three
minutes and 48 seconds would need to be
removed. Although this might seem like a
large number of cuts at first, many of the
cuts were very small.

Recognising that the film was intended as
a political allegory which intended - and
needed - to shock as part of its overall thesis,
the BBFC attempted to construct the cuts
carefully so that the message of the film, as
well as the meaning of each individual scene,
would be preserved.

However, the extent of the cuts did mean it
would be difficult, but not impossible, for
the distributor to make the necessary
changes and have the film classified in time

for the screening on August 29th 2010. In the event, the organisers of the Fright Fest decided they did not wish to screen a censored version of A Serbian Film, even if one could be prepared in time, and the screening was cancelled. Nonetheless, a cut version was prepared and submitted to the BBFC on October 21st 2010. This was checked by BBFC examiners and it was found that all requested cuts had been made although, in a few cases, scenes had been slightly overcut for continuity reasons. This version of the film - which had been cut by a total of four minutes and twelve seconds - met the BBFC's requirements and was classified at 18 without further cuts, on October 28th 2010. Even though the Board's intervention had lessened the impact of certain scenes, the cut version was still strong and disturbing and had the potential to upset and offend some viewers. This was reflected in the strong consumer advice of 'Contains very strong sexual violence, sex and violence'.

In the meantime, the film had been submitted to the BBFC for cinema release on September 22nd 2010. Initially, the distributor had hoped the BBFC might require fewer cuts for cinema release. However, the Board concluded that the same concerns applied for theatrical release and a cuts list, mirroring that issued for DVD and Blu-ray release was issued. The cut version was examined on November 23rd 2010 and was classified in the same BBFC-approved cut version on November 24th 2010.

Since then, the BBFC has received correspondence from people who were disappointed that 'A Serbian Film' had been cut, as well as from people who felt it should never have been classified at all. Some viewers of the cut version have written to the BBFC complaining they were disturbed by the cut version and that the BBFC intervention was insufficient. Subsequent attempts to screen the uncut version of the film at various locations around the UK have proven unsuccessful, with a number of local authorities taking Westminster's lead and refusing permission for the uncut version of the film to be shown, most notably in Bournemouth where a proposed screening in October at the Horror Film Festival was blocked. However, a single private screening did occur in London, as part of the Raindance Film Festival, in October 2010. The fact that this was a 'private event', with no admission being charged and to which only invited guests had access, meant that the local council felt it had no authority to prevent the screening taking place. Nonetheless, to date, there has been no public commercial screening of the uncut version of the film in the UK.

A SERBIAN FILM

It was some time before the BBFC revealed which scenes were cut from 'A Serbian Film'. The cuts made by the BBFC are as follows:

1. 01:45s. After Marija says to Miloš, Haven't we agreed about putting away your flicks?, remove all sight of the porn film on television immediately before it's switched off and we see Petar's reflection.

2. 35:15s. After shot of Miloš' face, remove entire shot in which we see Milos being fellated by Laylah while Jeca is seen on two screens in the background.

3. 35:30s. After shot of Miloš' face, remove entire shot of Jeca applying lipstick and licking her lips, whilst the watching Milos is being fellated.

4. 35:30s. After shot of Miloš' face, remove entire shot of Jeca with her mouth wrapped around the ice lolly and sucking it slowly, whilst the watching Miloš is being fellated.

5. 35:45s. After the implied ejaculation of Miloš into Laylah's mouth, remove the entire shot of Jeca licking the lolly stick and wiping the edges of her mouth and then smiling at Miloš mischievously, shrugging, and licking the lolly stick again.

6. 38:00s. After shot of Marko being fellated by woman, remove entire shot of Petar and his family on-screen, the source of Marko's sexual interest.

7. 38:30s. After shot of Marko being fellated by woman and the dialogue, Come, blow harder. Blow harder, remove entire shot of Petar and his mother blowing candles on birthday cake.

8. 38:30s. After shot of Marko being fellated by woman, remove entire shot of Petar with Marko and his family as Marko gives Petar a birthday present.

9. 38:45s. After shot of Marko's face, while continued fellatio is implied below screen, remove entire shot of Petar with his family as Miloš inhales helium from party balloon as the family laugh and which immediately precedes one of Miloš' porn films.

10. 44:15s. After sight of Jeca's mother lunging towards Miloš' crotch, remove the close shot of her grabbing Miloš' penis, taking it in her mouth, and biting down on the erect penis.

11. 44:15s. After shot of Miloš' being held around the neck, remove shot of Jeca leaning forward and smiling, exhibiting interest in the sexual violence.

12. 44:30s. After shot of man instructing Miloš to Hit the whore. Hit the whore!, remove close shot of Jeca's mother biting on Miloš' erect penis and following shot of Jeca

leaning towards the sexual violence and saying Hit her

13. 44:30s. After shot of man instructing Miloš to Hit her, remove shot of Jeca leaning towards the sexual violence and saying Hit her

14. 44:30s. After shots of Miloš' punching Jeca's mother in the face and following close shot of Miloš being held around the neck, remove sight of Jeca leaning forward and smiling at the sexual violence she's witnessing.

15. 45:00s. After close shot of Jeca's mother's face as she's vigorously masturbating Miloš, remove shot which follows directly and which reveals Jeca smiling at the violence and sex.

16. 45:15s. After close shot of Miloš being held around the neck, as we hear Jeca's mother gasping following Miloš' ejaculation

over her face, remove shot of Jeca leaning forward and smiling with satisfaction.

17. 47:45s. After close shot on Miloš' face, remove entire shot of man running his hand over, and groping and patting, the naked bruised buttocks of Jeca's mother in medium close shot, including pan up her naked body and sight of him lifting her heavily bloodied battered face.

18. 48:30s. After close shot of Miloš' face looking down, remove two shots of him turning the naked woman's body over with his foot, revealing her shaven genitals and her breasts covered in bruises, grazes and dried blood.

19. 48:45s. After shot on Miloš' face, distracted by the voice of his son calling out, Hit it, dad, tear it, dad, uncle Vukmir is shooting, remove shot of Milos turning, with

his penis in view, as his son sits in the background encouraging him to commit further acts of violence against the already bloodied and battered woman.

20. 56:00s. After shot of Miloš watching the screen, remove entire shot of man pulling down his underpants with baby held in position in front of his crotch.

21. 56:00s. After shot of Miloš watching the screen, remove entire shot showing the rape of the new-born baby, with sight of man with underpants partially pulled down as he thrusts into the struggling new-born baby held in front of his crotch.

22. 56:15s. After Vukmir turns to look at the watching Miloš, remove entire shot showing the rape of the new-born baby, with sight of man with underpants partially pulled down as he thrusts into the new-born baby held in front of his crotch.

23. 58:00s. In rapid montage, remove shot of new-born baby, in position in front of man's crotch, being raped.

24. 58:15s. In rapid montage, remove shot of Jeca sucking ice lolly intercut with the shots of Miloš' face (as he penetrates man's eye socket) and close shots of female genitals.

25. 58:15s. In rapid montage, remove close shot of Jeca's mother biting down on Miloš' erect penis.

26. 58:15s. In rapid montage, remove close shot of Jeca's mother lying naked, bruised and bloodied with breasts exposed.

27. 58:30s. In second rapid montage, remove all sight of heavily bloodied naked female body which appears to be that of the child, Jeca.

28. 63:00s. After Vukmir holds Miloš' face, remove sight of naked and chained mother of Jeca as she's dragged into room and thrown onto bed with some focus on her genitals and breasts.

29. 63:15s. After shot of man locking cuff to edge of bed, remove medium shot of Jeca's mother with naked buttocks raised towards camera and legs' pulled apart.

30. 63:45s. After shot of a sexually charged Miloš lunging towards Jeca's naked and restrained mother, remove sight of Jeca's mother naked and lying on the bed with her legs spread and raised to reveal shadowy shot of exposed genitals, as camera closes in on her buttocks and genitals.

31. 64:00s. After shot of Miloš raping Jeca's mother and accompanying dialogue from Vukmir, Sweet little Jeca watched her mother fuck the junky bums, remove

medium close profile shot of Jeca's mother being raped with focus on her breasts.

32. 64:15s. After shot of Miloš thrusting into Jeca's mother from behind, with focus on Jeca's mother's face and Vukmir's dialogue, ...who conceive babies in lust, remove medium shot of Miloš thrusting into Jeca's naked mother with full body detail as he continues to hit her; and subsequent shot of Miloš' continued raping as Jeca's mother looks back at him in fear, with breasts prominently swaying as Milos continues to beat her.

33. 64:30s. After shot on Jeca's mother's face and Vukmir's dialogue, Imagine her turning Petar into a dog-fucker's bitch!, remove second POV shot of Miloš' continued punching of Jeca's mother's naked back with focus on the heavy bruises which are being inflicted.

34. 65:00s. After shot of blood splattering onto picture on wall, remove close shots of

machete embedded into Jeca's mothers' neck and blood pumping from the wound.

35. 65:00s. After close shot of bloodied head being severed from heavily bloodied back, and Vukmir's dialogue, The unique magic of rigor mortis!, remove shot of Miloš thrusting into naked and heavily bloodied rear of the dead woman while holding the machete against her buttocks.

36. 65:15s. After shot of dead woman's torso pumping blood from neck, remove profile shot of Miloš continuing to thrust into dead woman's heavily bloodied rear while holding the machete against her buttocks.

37. 70:30s. After camcorder shot of teeth lying on the concrete in pool of blood, remove the close pan up a restrained Laylah's blood spattered naked body with focus on her bloodied breasts and heavily

A SERBIAN FILM

bloodied mouth with teeth having been
removed.

38. 71:15s. After close focus on masked
male's face, remove pan down to Laylah's
toothless and bloodied mouth as man
positions his erect penis in front of her face
and then forcefully penetrates her mouth
while holding the back of her head in
position.

39. 71:15s. After Miloš continues to look at
camcorder image, remove close shot of
erection forced into Laylah's mouth as her
head is firmly held in position.

40. 71:30s. After Miloš continues to look at
camcorder image, remove close shot of
continued deep thrusting of erect penis into
Laylah's bloodied mouth and sight of man
pinching her nose so that she is unable to
breath.

41. 71:30s. After Miloš continues to look at
camcorder image, remove close shot of

continued deep thrusting of erect penis into Laylah's bloodied mouth with accompanying pinching of her nose so that she is unable to breath.

42. 71:45s. After Miloš continues to look at camcorder image, remove close pan in on Laylah's bulging eyes as forced deep throat fellatio with nose pinching continues until Laylah dies, ending on pan down her dead body to close focus on her bloodied breasts as blood dribbles from her mouth onto her chest.

43. 74:00s. After close shot of Miloš' face, remove focus on Jeca as camera pans down to her putting her hand on Miloš' knee, accompanied by the dialogue, you'll have the honour of giving her a virgin's communion. To make her a woman

44. 74:30s. After Vukmir encourages Miloš to have sex with the child Jeca, with dialogue

A SERBIAN FILM

urging, Come on, come on..., remove close shot of Jeca encouraging Milos with her hand on his knee and trailing this up his thigh towards his groin; and following close shot on the child smiling at Miloš.

45. 83:15s. After Miloš is lead into the warehouse, remove sight of Petar's naked buttocks lying exposed next to those of his mother, on a bed, as camera pans in towards them.

46. 84:30s. After shot of Miloš thrusting into the fully covered child's body, remove close shot of Miloš' buttocks as he thrusts into his son while sitting over the child's naked legs.

47. 85:00s. After close shot of Miloš' face, remove close shot of Miloš' buttocks and scrotum as he thrusts against into his young son, forcing a mixture of blood and

excrement to squirt from the child's anus and down his thighs.

  48. 87:00s. After medium long shot of woman staggering into warehouse, remove close shot of her heavily bloodied crotch and thighs with metal pipe held next to her bloodied crotch.

  49. 87:15s. After shot of watching cameraman, remove close shot of woman's bloodied crotch and thighs, with pipe in her hand dripping blood, before she collapses to the floor.

DIRECTORS RESPONSE

The director and Writer of 'A Serbian Film' have been involved in several interviews concerning the films graphic portrayal of sexual violence, especially towards minors, and have been very vocal about their intent with the movie.

Spasojević and Radivojević, have since made statements to the effect that their creation is a parody of modern politically correct films made in Serbia which are financially supported by foreign funds.

A SERBIAN FILM

On the question, why 'Srpski Film' for the title, Radivojević answers: "We have become synonyms for chaos and lunacy. The title is a CYNICAL reference to that image. Srpski Film is also a metaphor for our national cinema — boring, predictable and altogether unintentionally hilarious which throughout our film to some extent is commented on and subtly parodied."

Similarly, Radivojević describes Serbian cinema as "...pathetic state financed films made by people who have no sense or connection to film, but are strongly supported by foreign funds. Quality of the film is not their concern, only the bureaucratic upholding of the rule book on political correctness."

According to Spasojević, the character of Vukmir is "an exaggerated representation of the new European film order ... the Western

A SERBIAN FILM

world has lost feelings, so they're searching for false ones, they want to buy feelings."

In another interview Spasojević is quoted as saying "my shocking 'A Serbian Film' denounces the fascism of political correctness." Questioned by the Croatian media on whether the violence depicted deals with crimes committed by Serbian soldiers during the Yugoslav Wars, Spasojević answered: "'Srpski Film' does not touch upon war themes, but in a metaphorical way deals with the consequences of post-war society and a man that is exploited to the extreme in the name of securing the survival of his family."

"As much as we try to deal with our life in this film allegorically, and with the corrupt political authorities that govern it, we are also dealing with today's Art and Cinema and the corrupt artistic authorities that govern them in a similar manner here. The films that preach and enforce political correctness are the dominant form of cinematic expression today. Nowadays in Eastern Europe you cannot get a film financed unless you have a pathetic and heart-warming 'true story' to tell about some poor lost refugee girls with matchsticks, who ended up as victims of war, famine and/or intolerance. They mostly deal with VICTIMS as heroes, and they use and manipulate them in order to activate the viewer's empathy. They make a false, romanticized story about that victim and sell it as real life. That is real pornography and manipulation, and also spiritual violence – the cinematic fascism of political correctness."

Spasojević and Radivojević also express that the film is not exclusively dealing with Serbian issues but issues in the "New World" in general. "We didn't want to make a

A SERBIAN FILM

hermetic picture that would deal exclusively with our local tragedies, but to tell a story with global overtones, because Serbia is merely a reflection of the ways of today's New World in general, as it tries to imitate it and fails miserably. Contrary to the peerless politically correct facade of the New World, it's still a soulless devouring machine for killing every small freedom – of art and free speech – we have left, destroying everything different in its path."

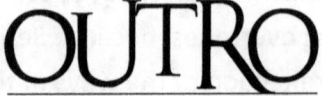

'A Serbian Film' has had a clear impact on the world, whether we like it or not, and in turn has earned a place in the history of cinema. However, as hard as it may be to believe, its presence was over shadowed by 'The human Centipede', making it more of a modern cult classic than a modern day right of passage.

While the movie remains banned in several countries, and heavily cut in others, there are legitimate uncut releases on Blu-Ray & DvD. These releases can often be found on eBay, or are readily available from third party sellers on websites like Amazon.

Personally, I believe that 'A Serbian Film' is an underrated, artistically expressive, and very important film. I hold it in higher regards than others will, and I highly recommend that if you have the stomach for watching a disturbing movie like this, then go ahead and watch it. But before you do it is best to remember that once you have seen 'A Serbian Film' you cannot unsee it!

Other Books From VIDEOGEDDON:

Guinea Pig: The Darker Side Of Japanese
Cinema by Fwah Storm

Coming Soon From VIDEOGEDDON:

Sadist Cinema: Bad Lieutenant

Sadist Cinema: Men Behind The Sun

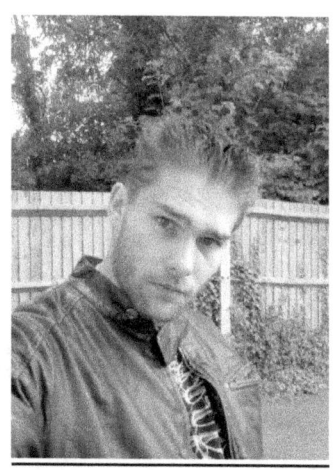

Other Books by Fwah Storm:

Svengali

The Fallen: Between Angels & Insects

The Asylum of Fables: Volume One

Guinea Pig: The Darker Side of Japanese Cinema

Coming Soon – Djent

Coming Soon – The Fallen: Renaissance

Connect with Fwah Storm:

www.fwahstorm.co.uk

twitter.com/fwahstorm

www.facebook.com/officialfwahstorm

www.reloadcomics.co.uk

www.facebook.com/thefallenbookseries

*Don't forget to rate and review this book on
Amazon & Goodreads.com*